# The Grace Process Guidebook

# The Grace Process
# Guidebook

A practical guide for
transcending your ego and
engaging the wisdom of your heart

Lori Leyden, Ph.D., M.B.A.

CREATE GLOBAL HEALING PRESS

SANTA BARBARA, CALIFORNIA

www.TheGraceProcess.com

Published by Create Global Healing Press
Santa Barbara, California

Cover photo by Gene Rosen,
who offered shelter and comfort
to the first students to escape the tragedy
at Sandy Hook Elementary School
on December 14, 2012

Editing and interior design by Jan Allegretti

ISBN-13: 978-1490438108
ISBN-10: 1490438106

To my original Grace Angels
in Santa Barbara and Rwanda,
who were courageous enough
to embrace Grace

# Table of Contents

# Part I

# Finding Grace

*The future belongs to those who believe
in the beauty of their dreams.*

–Eleanor Roosevelt

# Our Hearts Have the Answers

Imagine there is a computer system for activating that part of our DNA that hardwires us for divinity. The hardware is the heart and the software is gratitude, love, joy, and wonder. Once activated, this system gives us maximum speed for connecting with the Universal Internet where the Divine One Heart exists.

Now imagine seven billion people with seven billion hearts and at least seven billion passions. Imagine billions of hearts beating within the Divine One Heart with compassion and shared visions for peace, safety, and abundance for all. If we simply connected with each other and organized ourselves through our common passions, what possibilities might unfold?

This is the possibility and the promise of The Grace Process, that each of us will learn to receive the healing we yearn for so we can find true peace and contentment within our own hearts, and live the lives we were meant to lead. And when a critical mass of people operates from this heart-centered paradigm, we can then fulfill our collective divine purpose to generate the evolution of peace on our planet.

## Living in the Nightmare or the Dream

The Grace Process™ (TGP) is a spiritual practice based on the principle that your deepest healing is possible when you resonate with the energy of Grace. The practice focuses on clearing the mental, emotional, and spiritual blockages that are generated by your ego, and that interfere with your ability to receive Grace. With TGP you will learn to:

- lift out of your judgments and the "ego stories" you use to define who you are;
- open to forgiveness;
- hold an expanded heart resonance of gratitude, love, joy, and wonder; and
- receive the healing you desire.

Most of us block our ability to receive Grace and live within an illusion of separation from the Divine because we live instead within the world of the ego. Our ego's survival defense is chauvinism, which I define as our judgments and our resistance to forgiveness—of others, ourselves, and the circumstances in which we find ourselves. We are locked in a "suffer and struggle" paradigm of growing, changing, and learning our life lessons—not only on a personal level but on a global level as well. As individuals, as a nation, and as a world, many of us are burdened with a crisis of spirit. Frozen in the nightmare of what is wrong, we no longer have the passion, desire, and imagination to dream bigger dreams for ourselves and our planet. In other words, we are more attached to our "nightmare stories" than we are to our "dream stories."

As I write this our world is rich with opportunity to attach to nightmare stories. So many of us are facing severe health, career, and financial challenges; our economy and our personal finances are in serious crisis; issues of sexism, racism, and greed are front and center; scandals of all kinds are emerging; devastating natural disasters arise without warning; we are in the middle of seemingly endless wars all around the globe as well as in our inner cities; and the faces of all those who are suffering inhuman conditions plague us in the news every day.

It's true, these are most assuredly urgent issues that demand our attention. However, we must learn to recognize whether we are viewing these circumstances through our egos or through our hearts.

When we view our life circumstances through the ego we feed the ego's addiction to judgment, control, fear, and hopelessness. It becomes easier than ever to get caught up in the melodrama of our stories, to "go unconscious," to be seduced into the trance state of a victim mentality. In this state we only see the nightmare of what this life can be. Once triggered, these ego addictions feed on themselves like a cancer, perpetuating the same frequencies that created those issues in the first place. As

Einstein taught us, *we can't solve a problem from the level on which it was created.* The energy of these addictions does not and cannot empower us to co-create miracles that will resolve our current problems.

What if we could operate within a very different perspective on these issues, one that allows us to live the dream of all the wonder and beauty that this life can be? What if every individual, circumstance, and condition we encounter had the potential to assist us in our healing and to help us to discover the true power that lies within our very own hearts?

*What if the complexity and intensity of today's issues, in our personal lives and in our world, are not nightmares at all, but in fact are the voice of the Divine One Heart calling us home— calling us home to our truer selves, to our divine selves?*

If this becomes the lens of our perception, then from this place of connecting with our divinity we can come together to co-create a higher resonance that enables loving and harmonious solutions to unfold. That is, we will at last be able to co-create miracles and gifts, based on cooperation and sharing of resources, to manifest a world where anyone who chooses to can live in the dream—and it all begins in that place inside our hearts, where we feel at home with ourselves.

## The Global Shift Has Already Begun

All around us, if we choose to focus our lens of perception in the right places, we can see signs that this co-creation has already begun. Grace-filled communities around the globe are manifesting the dream of a more peaceful, safer, more abundant world.

- The HeartMath Institute has launched its Global Coherence Initiative, committed to planetary harmony and healing. To date, ten thousand people in fifty-six countries around the world have signed up to learn skills for raising heart resonance and using the power of their hearts for peaceful resolutions to world conflicts.

- In his book *Blessed Unrest: How the Largest Movement in the World Came into Being and Why No One Saw It Coming,* Paul Hawken documents the largest emergence of diverse, innovative, and heart-centered strategies the world has ever seen, with more than 130,000 social and environmental change organizations in existence in the world right now. He describes this phenomenon as humanity's collective genius, an unstoppable movement to reimagine our relationship with ourselves, one another, and the environment.

- In 1972 the Himalayan country of Bhutan established a Gross National Happiness (GNH) index to measure its strength. Despite the strife and hardship this tiny country has experienced over the years, its current leader, His Majesty King Jigme Khesar Namgyel Wangchuck, continues to lead his nation by including citizens' mental and emotional health among measures of its development. Whatever the goals of his country are, King Khesar knows that without peace, security, and happiness, he, his people, and his nation have nothing.

Representatives from governments across the globe attended last year's fourth annual GNH conference.

- As of this writing, students from Pacific Grove Middle School and their teacher, Moira Mahr, have developed the first student humanitarian program associated with Create Global Healing, a non-profit organization that fosters heart-centered leadership development. The students call themselves the Children2Children Project. In less than one year these sixth- and seventh-graders have created a Peace Quilt project that  now includes quilt sections from Rwandan and Nicaraguan orphans; a letter writing and peace mandala campaign, gathering gifts I can deliver to orphans I work with in Rwanda; and a song about why we should care about orphans around the world. They've also raised more than $2,200 to provide food and fresh water for their Rwandan brothers and sisters. And all of this came straight from their own hearts with no prompting from adults.

## Evidence of the Dream

We are now seeing a remarkable convergence of science and spirituality, as the scientific community begins to see proof of what spiritual luminaries have known for millennia. Marilyn Schlitz, Cassandra Vieten, and Tina Amorak of the Institute for Noetic Sciences, Doc Lew Childre of the HeartMath Institute, David Hawkins, Gregg Braden, and Joseph Chilton Pearce are just of few of the leaders in this field who have conducted groundbreaking research or written extensively about it. Here is just a sample of what we've learned from them:

8

- The *first cells* to form when you were a fetus were in your heart.
- Your heart began to beat *before* your brain was formed.
- The human heart produces the hormone atrial natriuretic factor, or ANF, which influences the immune system and the structure and function of the brain, in particular the limbic system, where emotions, stress response, memory, and learning take place.
- The heart has its own neural cells that are identical to brain cells—in effect, *the heart has its own brain.* Neural cells in the heart monitor and influence all the functions of the body, brain, and mind. They govern the interactions between the heart and the emotional and cognitive structures of the brain.
- A negative emotional state brings an automatic shift of attention and energy away from the higher verbal-intellectual brain toward the lower reptilian brain and its defenses. This shift shortchanges the intellect, cripples learning and memory, and puts higher brain functions under the control of the reptilian brain.
- A positive emotional state shifts concentration and energy toward the higher brain functions in the prefrontal cortex. Through this mechanism the heart can influence advanced intellectual skills *as well as the higher human virtues of love, understanding, and compassion.*
- When we change the way we feel about what's happened to us in our past, our body chemistry changes in the present. *This is what happens when we practice forgiveness.*

- Spiritual endeavor and intention change the brain function and the body's physiology, and establish *a specific area of spiritual information in the right-brain prefrontal cortex.*

- There is a field of energy that connects all of creation. This field is holographic, meaning that every part of it is connected to every other part, and each piece mirrors the whole on a smaller scale. Therefore, our individual choices combine to become our collective reality. *We choose our reality.*

- We communicate with the holographic energy field through the language of emotion. Negative emotions connect with negative energy in the field; positive emotions connect with positive energy in the field.

- In studies using applied kinesiology to measure states of consciousness, researchers have demonstrated that *gratitude, love, joy, and wonder are the emotions most likely to give rise to transformation, inner peace, and enlightenment.*

- Studies conducted by the International Peace Project confirmed what is referred to as the "Maharishi Effect." When a small percentage of any population—the square root of one percent—achieved inner peace through meditation, that peace was reflected in the rest of the community in the form of reduced crime, acts of terrorism, traffic accidents, and emergency room visits. *Enough people, focused on shared intention, practicing gratitude, love, joy and wonder can change the world.*

It's more and more clear that our hearts truly are the hardware that connects us with the Divine One Heart, and that the language of the Divine One Heart is in fact gratitude, love, joy, and wonder. We really do have the answers and the means to bring about personal and global peace.

## An Invitation to Choose

We have before us at this time in our world an invitation grounded in the greatest of our divine gifts, our free will. The essence of free will is our divine power of *choice*. Put simply, the invitation is this:

*Do you choose to live in the nightmare of what life can be
or in the dream of what life can be?*

The Grace Process will give you the tools to recognize whether you are engaging the world through your ego and all its illusions or immersing yourself in the gratitude, love, joy, and wonder generated by your heart. With TGP you will learn how to *choose* heart resonance moment by moment, day by day, so you can experience the miracles and gifts all around you, connect with your divinity, and live the dream of what this life can be.

# From Soul Myth to Sacred Story:
# The Grace of Receiving

I know as well as anyone what it's like to live in the world of the ego, filled with judgment of myself and others, unable to break out of the pattern of stories and dramas spinning in my head. My own personal soul myth—you know, those illusions we come into this lifetime to heal—evolved from my beliefs that "dreams don't come true," "love isn't safe," "I am alone," and "I am unalterably flawed and undeserving of peace and happiness." These were the perceptions that fed my ego stories and ultimately blocked my ability to receive the transformational healing I most wanted.

A secret chamber in my heart began to open in the fall of 2003. In the space of eight weeks I left my marriage, my home, and my business, and underwent two emergency surgeries. While in the hospital for the second surgery I had a near death experience. My ego had a survival plan that I now know would have kept me locked into old paradigms that clearly were not working for me. The antidote to the hold my ego had over me came most unexpectedly while I was in the hospital, when in a critical moment I learned to receive the help I so desperately needed.

I had been hospitalized and in intense pain for three weeks. I'd lost twenty percent of my body weight, and was so weak that every breath was an effort. In the wee hours of the morning I began to feel a floating sensation; it seemed as though I was meeting myself and the energy of the Divine, in a space just outside and above my body. That's when I heard, or felt, these words:

*Everything in life is a choice,*
*including taking the next breath.*

In the quiet wonder of the moment I moved into the experience of not taking the next breath. I was no longer aware of pain, just relief and a calm well-being beyond time and space.

My reverie was suddenly broken when I heard my eighty-year-old roommate say, in a loud voice from the other side of the curtain, "Dear God, please help my roommate. She's really, really sick!"

It was startling, to say the least. I felt the urge to laugh, and thought, *This is no divine hint. This is an out loud miracle!* The next thing I knew, my urge to laugh forced a gasp of air into my lungs and *boom!* I was back in my body.

The following morning a new nurse appeared in my room. It was Jenny, a client I'd worked with more than thirteen years before. She said, "I remember what you did to help me, and I'm going to stay with you until we figure out how to get you better."

Jenny's first order of business was to get me cleaned up. I hadn't been bathed in three weeks, my drainage tube wasn't working properly, my incision dressing had not been changed in a week, and I had been vomiting for two days. You would think that my desire for help would have overridden any embarrassment I might have felt. But as Jenny gently peeled the hospital johnnie off of me in the bathroom, all I could feel was overwhelming shame for having to be in such a position of helplessness. I was especially mortified to have a former client see me this way.

Just as I was feeling an intensity of shame I didn't know possible, my humiliation dissolved into a miracle of receiving that I had never before experienced. In that Grace-filled moment I understood the power of receiving help without fear, judgment, or shame. I was finally able to open my heart to my own worthiness, and to the ultimate freedom of receiving love and care that was safe—and so necessary.

Amazing as it seems even to me, it took those absolutely desperate circumstances to finally break down my defenses and open my heart to the mystery of what pure love is—an unbroken, unending circuit of giving and receiving. The Grace of this miracle of receiving continues to unfold for me.

## The Birth of The Grace Process

That moment in the hospital with Jenny, in the midst of that tumultuous time, set me on a new trajectory. Despite the chaos within and surrounding me, in every area of my life, I continued to learn lessons about receiving the Grace to be in the quiet stillness of my heart to look for answers.

That's how I received The Grace Process. After my near death experience I became aware of a deeper sense of connectedness and clarity in my meditations and a heightened sense of intuition throughout the day. It was as if I could "download" the answers I was looking for right into my heart. Since one of my greatest passions was finding ways to help people heal their grief and trauma more elegantly, I made a significant choice to download the next level of my healing work. One morning, in deep meditation, I received my intention—and The Grace Process was born.

I knew it was time to trust my heart to lead me.

That trust carried me from one coast across the country to another, from one professional paradigm to a new one, and ultimately nine thousand miles around the world to come home to more of myself and the power of my heart. It was a journey that changed everything I thought I knew about the world and my place in it. I was able to see beyond the illusions of my ego, and discover a whole new way to live my life—a whole new set of choices. This is what I learned:

*The more I open my heart to myself and experience*
*receiving as much as giving, the more I can allow myself to*
*be carried by the miracles and gifts in my life and the easier*

16

*it is to discover more of my personal service work and my*
*work of service in the world.*

## The Grace Process in Rwanda

At no time has this been clearer to me than in the time I spend each year on the other side of the globe doing trauma healing work with survivors of the worst of human tragedies. Amazingly, I experience the essence of Grace itself in the eyes and hearts of the Rwandan genocide survivors I work with, women and children who have endured and continue to live with the most horrific of human suffering.

I remember one of my first meetings with a widow whose husband and children were murdered, and her own rape had left her living in poverty with AIDs. She showed me her mutilated chest, part of the torture of her rape. In that moment I knew the only thing I had to offer was to be as fully and completely present in my heart as I could possibly be, and to allow my heart to lead me. There was no translator, so we spoke with our eyes. We brought our hands to one another's hearts until the moment felt complete.

While I could easily have descended into the distraction of feeling absolutely inadequate and desperate to do something helpful, I knew we were giving and receiving from our hearts, and for the time being our presence with each other was enough.

During these visits to Rwanda I have the great honor of using The Grace Process to facilitate trauma healing work with orphan genocide survivors. They are adolescents, boys and girls

17

aged fifteen to twenty-four, living in extreme poverty. Many of them are orphan heads of households, raising two or as many as six other orphans. Regardless of the intensity of the traumas we deal with—poverty, rape, torture, mutilation, disease, murder, hopelessness, and despair—these orphans enthusiastically and sincerely engage in exercises to find peace and hope in their bodies, their hearts, and their lives.

I begin our work together with some basic trauma healing techniques. Once they are able to experience some inner safety they are surprisingly eager to embrace the practice of being in gratitude, love, joy, and wonder. As I take them through the steps of The Grace Process, what unfolds is always beyond my imagination. They find creative solutions for how they will work together to help other traumatized orphans. They find and share resources, come to understand the freedom of forgiveness, and feel more connected to the Divine at work in their lives. The power of giving and receiving the love and compassion we share with each other expands my vision for transforming our world.

Ultimately these young people show me the magnitude of what The Grace Process can do—not just for you and for me as individuals, but also for the healing of our planet. What if the radical solution for these radical times is all about expanding our own heart resonance so that one by one we can create a vibration so powerful, a critical mass of others will also be transformed? Perhaps then, in the spirit of cooperation and harmony, we can generate those radically creative solutions that can lift us and our world out of the destructive dramas currently being played out in so many ways.

What got me to Rwanda? Trusting what made my heart sing. What makes the work effective? A spirit of hope and dignity, seeing the divinity in ourselves and one another, and opening our hearts to each other. Is it enough? No, but it is a beginning.

## A Dream for Our World

Imagine what's possible when a critical mass of people begins to live within that paradigm. With all those people living their dreams for our world, and all those hearts beating as one within the Divine One Heart—a global shift toward heart resonance seems inevitable. If it's true that the minimum number of people required to jump-start a change in consciousness is the square root of one percent of a population, that means it only takes 8,366 people in the entire world to begin the transformation!

Before The Grace Process I was caught in the cycle of suffer-and-struggle, a victim of the stories generated by my ego, lost in the illusion of separation from myself and from the Divine. After my experiences with TGP I know that the only love that needs to feel safe is the love I have for myself, and that dreams really do come true if I dare to dream them from an open heart. Now my personal soul myth has been replaced by my personal sacred story, which evolves around an entirely new set of beliefs. I now know that "I have and will have all the resources I need to fulfill my destiny," "love is safe because I love myself," "my heart connects me to the Divine One Heart," and "I am discovering more and more of my divinity every day."

Most important of all, I know that as I live my personal sacred story, and share the gifts of The Grace Process with you, together we begin to generate a critical mass of people operating from this heart-centered paradigm—and I hold the certainty that this is the way for peace to evolve on our planet.

# The Heart's True Wisdom

Here's what I now know and live from in my heart. Even though what follows may not be new to you—nor is it new to me—what is different for me now is that I have taken these truths from my intellect and placed them in my heart where I can experience them and live them more elegantly and easily.

- Separation from myself, others, nature, and the Divine is the grandest illusion we are here in physical form to heal.

- Our egos, in the form of judgment and resistance to forgiveness, are our central defense, holding the illusion of separation in place.

- Our greatest human gift is choice.

- Our egos block our gift of choice.
- Our hearts are the ultimate vehicle of connectedness.
- Our hearts are wired to resonate with the highest of all human frequencies.
- The highest human frequencies are gratitude, love, joy, and wonder.
- Freed from our egos, our hearts will choose to resonate with gratitude, love, joy, and wonder.
- Gratitude, love, joy, and wonder combine to create the highest resonance for receiving and harnessing divine Grace.
- Grace is powered by the eternal infinity circuit of giving and receiving.

- Seeking and becoming one with our divinity is the purest choice for our *en-lighten-ment.*
- When we open our hearts to ourselves we are in service to becoming our divine selves.
- As we experience the Grace of our divine selves, our hearts yearn to be in service to the divinity in others, nature, and the Divine One Heart.
- There is no true Grace without simultaneously giving and receiving.
- Being in service to myself and the Divine One Heart is the ultimate human expression of giving and receiving.

- Our hearts resonate internally and externally with the Divine One Heart.

- As each human heart seeks itself in connectedness with the Divine One Heart, Grace can envelop our world and the field of all possibilities can unfold.

The Grace Process is a treasure map for exploring, discovering, and living these inherent truths from your own heart.

## Reclaiming Our Divine Birthright

Over the past five thousand years we have been graced with many enlightened teachers and healers guiding us to love ourselves and to find peace in our hearts so we can create peace in our world. I am deeply grateful and in awe of the heart-centered resonance they have brought to the planet, and for the way the impact of their presence has allowed us to evolve as spiritual beings.

Because of their example and heart mastery we are very close to a tipping point at which enough of us, committed to the same heart-centered vision and values, can choose enlightenment and lift ourselves globally to another level of reality. I believe we can move beyond our mystical yearnings for enlightenment to realize and experience it in a way never before seen on our planet.

No matter where your spiritual adventures have taken you or what spiritual practices you engage in, The Grace Process can be an elegant practice to complement whatever is already working for you. It will,

- activate and elevate your spiritual journey to a whole new level of fun and wonder, beyond what you had imagined it could be;

- provide a practical yet deep map for connecting you with a heart resonance that helps you lift out of your stories, open to forgiveness, and hold an expanded awareness in your heart of gratitude, love, joy, and wonder so you are open to receiving the healing you desire;

- enable you to resonate at higher and higher levels of gratitude, love, joy, and wonder so that you become a vibrational match with Grace. In those feeling states you become one with your divinity and connectedness with the Divine One Heart, your healing flows more elegantly.

But first we must fall in love with ourselves and our world as we are now. From this open-hearted place of nonresistance to what is, we can begin the work of healing ourselves and our world. As we allow ourselves to pursue our heart's desires we ignite a spark that activates those codes in our DNA that hardwire us to our divinity, and we expand our ability to give and receive love. With each individual spark, we ignite a greater flame of resonance that calls others to join us in our shared visions and values.

With that dream in our hearts, I'd like to share with you my personal prayer for peace:

My God is your God

My religion is gratitude, love, joy, and wonder

When I am:

One with my Breath

One with my Body

One with my Heart

One with my World

We can be:

One with our Breath

One with our Bodies

One with our Hearts

One with our World

# Part II

# The Grace Process:

## Putting It into Practice

*You are intimately connected to all things in the universe.*
*You do make a difference in the world.*
*By harnessing the transformative power of Grace*
*you become a beacon of light and healing*
*for yourself and our world.*

*Now envision a world in which everyone*
*is living his or her divinity.*

# The Grace Process Formula

The Grace Process (TGP) is based on five elements of healing: intention, releasing judgment, forgiveness, heart resonance, and receiving and harnessing Grace. In the pages that follow you'll learn how each element works, why it's so powerful, and how you can choose to incorporate all of them into your daily life. Once you do, you will begin to heal in ways you never thought possible, more quickly than you imagined you could, and you'll discover how you can finally live the life you came here to live.

Why is this practice so powerful? TGP creates a new paradigm for transformation because it addresses what I believe are the most essential wounds that all of us—individuals, communities, and our world—need to heal. For each of these essential wounds TGP offers an alternative that you can choose in place of your woundedness, an alternative that resonates with the energy of Grace.

The following table lists the essential wounds we all share, and the healing that is available if we choose to embrace it.

| THE ESSENTIAL WOUND: | WITH TGP YOU CAN CHOOSE TO: |
| --- | --- |
| **The wound of separation,** the feeling that you're alone, disconnected from yourself, others, and the world | **Open your heart to your divinity,** and experience your connection to the Divine One Heart. |
| **Living in the "suffer and struggle" mode,** believing that you must simply endure life's challenges no matter how difficult they seem | **Heal with elegance and ease,** and find the healing available to you within each challenge. |
| **Self-abandonment,** ignoring your needs and wants in favor of what you believe others require of you, or because you believe you are unworthy | **Love yourself with healthy boundaries,** and learn to recognize and honor your emotions as valuable guides to your own healing. |

| | |
|---|---|
| **Religious wounds**, the misguided teachings and practices that lead you away from your own divinity | **Allow your spirituality to come alive** in every moment of your life. |
| **Chauvinism**, the judgments of yourself, others, and your circumstances that make you a victim of your ego | **Open your heart** to cooperation, harmony, peace, and abundance for yourself, for others, and for the world. |

TGP "Technology" is a roadmap for you to follow in making your personal and collective shift to apply new healing paradigms to these essential wounds. There are three steps in the process:

1. Make a fundamental choice to heal with Grace by practicing the five elements of the TGP formula.
2. Develop strategies that will keep you on the track of transcending your ego so you can experience more elegant, heart-conscious healing.
3. Incorporate the principles of TGP into your everyday life so that your spirituality infuses every moment, every choice, every miracle, and you experience the transformation that will bring about peace in your heart and peace in our world.

## The Fundamental Choice to Heal with Grace

Choosing Grace as your path toward healing marks the beginning of your journey. The most powerful and elegant way to receive Grace, and resonate the energy of Grace each and every day, is to choose to be in gratitude, love, joy, and wonder in as many moments as possible. From that place, everything you perceive and everything you encounter has the potential to be a miracle or a gift in service to your healing and fulfillment as a spiritual adventurer.

## What Is Grace?

Grace is the transcendent experience of remembering your oneness. That sense of oneness or connectedness can be with yourself, other people, nature, and the Divine One Heart. When we are in Grace we are aware of the divine truth, goodness, and beauty in whatever we are experiencing, and in that moment the ordinary becomes extraordinary. We experience Grace when we are at one with our divinity. In Grace, our ego and sense of separation dissolve into a resonance of harmony and peace with the Divine One Heart.

We have been taught to believe that Grace is beyond our control, and that it's an unmerited favor from God that we don't deserve and can't earn. All of this leads us to believe that Grace is an uncertain experience that we can never anticipate. Before I discovered the power of gratitude, love, joy, and wonder, my own experiences of Grace occurred in elusive moments of deep despair and fear, in prolonged states of meditation or prayer, or in transitory communion with nature or another person.

Looking back on those moments I can say that Grace occurred because I dropped my ego defenses and, through exhaustion, complete confusion, or a return to innocence, I opened my heart to receive.

After working with The Grace Process, I now know that Grace arises with certainty when we meet the Divine in the field of the Divine. What is the field of the Divine? I believe it is a field of resonance that, as humans, we experience when our hearts vibrate at the highest possible frequencies. We generate those frequencies when we experience gratitude, love, joy, and wonder, and together they create the attractor resonance for Grace. In that state we connect with the same resonance in the Divine One Heart and become divine co-creators of the miracles and gifts we want to bring into our lives.

When we live in and from our egos, when we resonate with negativity and judgment, we block experiences of Grace. TGP offers a way to move beyond our egos and resonate with the energy of Grace—whenever we choose to do so.

In my life and work I have found experiences of Grace to be unique to each individual and yet connected by some common threads that weave those experiences together. Grace can feel transcendent in different ways. Sometimes it is joyful, energetic, and active—more masculine or "spirit-full." At other times it may be quiet, yet expansively touching and tender—more feminine or "soul-full." Or, it can simply be a deep sense of knowing, perhaps more "higher-self-full."

There's a difference between having an experience of Grace and allowing those experiences to inspire healing that is transformative and life changing. The difference lies in your ability to choose to allow the miracles and gifts of Grace to be real. Transformation comes about when you:

- acknowledge with gratitude, love, joy, and wonder that your intention for healing is unfolding;
- allow your perception of yourself to change, so that you see more of your divinity as a result of that healing;
- act from that place of healing in your heart.

The more you experience the transformative power of Grace the easier it will be for you to experience the dream of what this life can be. As you learn to find gratitude, love, joy, and wonder in every present moment you'll come to know how truly supported you are by the Divine One Heart. You will know how to trust the wisdom of your heart for answers, and your relationships, your passions, your creativity, your abundance, your work, your health—everything will flow more easily and elegantly.

Each time you choose to receive Grace and be transformed by it you are co-creating new maps for healing yourself and our world.

## TGP Formula for Choosing Grace

The TGP formula for harnessing the energy of Grace is relatively straightforward. It begins and ends with the choice to make the following five elements of healing part of your everyday life:

1. **Intention:** Choose to live in the beauty and wonder of what this life was meant to be, and create the most expansive intentions for manifesting the healing or miracle you desire.

2. **Releasing judgment:** Become aware of any and all judgments you may have about yourself, others, and the circumstances in which you find yourself. Pay particular attention to those that relate to your intentions.

3. **Forgiveness:** Forgive yourself, others, and the circumstances in which you find yourself. Pay particular attention to issues that are related to your intentions.

4. **Heart resonance:** Hold within your heart the highest resonance of gratitude, love, joy and wonder (GLJW) in as many moments as possible as you co-create your intentions. These are the highest frequencies for attracting and harnessing Grace.

5. **Receiving and harnessing Grace:** Receive and honor the miracles and gifts all around you as you live in the energy of Grace. Welcome the transformation of your healing and the realization of your intentions.

---

### TGP Formula for Choosing to Heal with Grace

(Intention) (- Judgments + Forgiveness) (Heart Resonance)

= Receiving and Harnessing Grace

---

## Intention

Whether you call it a prayer, an affirmation, or an intention, the underlying purpose is the same: to focus your awareness and call into your life something you desire. You can set healing intentions for every aspect of your mental, emotional, physical and spiritual life—for your relationships with yourself and others; for your work, health and finances; for what you want to achieve, experience, and know; for the healing of others; and for the healing of our planet. All intentions are healing intentions. Even when you desire to achieve something like financial success you are essentially asking to heal anything in your ego that is blocking you from that achievement.

Start simply, with just one or a few intentions that are a priority for you. As you become familiar with the process your heart will lead you to continue in the right direction. The more you live in your heart and the more Grace you experience, the more intentions you will want to set for yourself and our world.

To facilitate the realization of your desires, it's important to focus on the evidence that your healing is unfolding. As you work with the TGP formula you'll see more and more hints and clues that your healing has already begun. You may find yourself changing the focus of your intentions as you drop your judgments and open to forgiveness. Keep a journal of the miracles and gifts that show up in your life in general and as they relate to your healing. It's a great way to recognize how your healing has progressed, and whether it's time to set a more expanded intention or create entirely new ones.

As we know, science has now proven that we are active participants with the universe in co-creating what we desire. How does it work? The real secret to co-creation lies in these two simple steps:

- Focus on what it is that you truly desire.
- With gratitude, love, joy, and wonder, feel that what you desire is already on its way to you.

**Focus on what you truly desire.** Oftentimes when we set an intention for healing, our language is focused on what we don't want in our lives rather than on what we do want. For example, your intention might be *I want to heal my depression.* This puts your attention and feeling state on your depression rather than on your healing. If you put your focus on what you do want, you might state your intention this way: *I embrace hope and happiness.*

A critical component of setting an intention is to identify the difference between the *form* of what you desire and the *function* it would have in your life, and then build your intention around the function rather than the form. Let's look at an example. Most of us want more money, and are focused on having it so we can buy what we desire. But money is just one form, one avenue for manifesting what we desire. If you understand what you want money to do for you, its function, and build your intention around that, you may find that what shows up is far more elegant than you could have imagined.

To discover the function of what you truly want, ask yourself, "What do I want the money (or a bigger house, or a better job, or a spouse) to do for me?" Do you want it to make you feel successful, or safe? If that's the case, then focus your intention on achieving success or safety. You might discover that you receive opportunities that may or may not bring you more money, but that bring you far more success, confidence, self-esteem, and feelings of inner safety than you ever hoped to find. Of course, once you receive what you desire, it's up to you to recognize the function of what you asked for no matter what form it comes in.

Let's look at one more example. This one demonstrates the difference between asking for what you want versus what you don't want, and also how to ask for the function rather than the form of your intention. Consider the intention *I release my addiction to food (or alcohol, shopping, melodrama)*. This might be a good place to start, but it is focused on what you don't want instead of what you do want, and also on the form rather than the function of your intention. Ask yourself, "What will I have the freedom to experience when my addiction is healed?" Then ask, "What do I want the freedom from addiction to do for me?" Your answer might be, "I'll have the freedom to enjoy being in my heart in the present moment." And so, a more positive intention, with a more expansive heart resonance, might be *I embrace being in my heart in the present moment.*

As you can see, in this case we've examined whether you're seeking *freedom from* something or the *freedom to have* what you desire. When you focus on the freedom to have what you desire your heart feels joyful, open, expansive, while focusing on a wish to be free from something you dislike makes your heart feel negative, dark, contracting. You can also see how releasing the

38

form of your intention invites something far more expansive than a smaller-sized pair of jeans. It opens the door to receiving the gift of being heart-centered in every moment—and all the healing that can emerge from that.

**Feel that what you desire is already on its way.** As we're learning from quantum physics, we communicate with the Divine field through our emotions. Positive emotions connect with positive energy in the Divine One Heart. As you connect with the feelings of already having what you desire, you begin the manifestation process. You can trust that your healing will continue to unfold as long as you avoid the distractions— judgments and resistance to forgiveness—of your ego.

Imagine how you will feel when you have the healing you seek:

- What will you feel?
- How will you act?
- Who and what will be in your life that isn't present now?
- How will you spend your days?
- What miracles and gifts will unfold in your world?

As you practice feeling these things in your body, pay attention to the miracles and gifts that appear. Can you find the clues that your healing is already unfolding in your reality?

## Releasing Judgment

The stories and dramas our ego plays out for us are generally a form of judgment. The essential wound of separation—the illusion that we are alone and disconnected from our divinity—leads us to be critical of ourselves, others, or the circumstances in which we find ourselves. In all cases we objectify that which we judge, perpetuating the illusion of separation and interfering with our ability to take responsibility for ourselves. When we are in judgment of ourselves, it carries the added burden of self-abandonment. Ultimately we become our own abusers.

It's helpful to recognize that judgment is a form of chauvinism, which encompasses any attachment to being right or being perfect, and any motivation or effort to control, manipulate, exploit, dominate, gain power over, blame, shame, or withhold forgiveness from ourselves or another. The feeling of entitlement, or of being "better than," is an indication of chauvinism against others, while feeling "less than," or unworthy, indicates chauvinism against ourselves.

In order to understand the impact and limitations of chauvinism or judgment we need to understand that they create a very powerful physiological reaction in the body. Any time we operate from that illusion of separation, we generate fear that activates our lower reptilian brain, putting us in survival mode as hormones such as adrenalin, cortisol, and other steroids are pumped throughout the body. Activation of our reptilian brain also interferes with our ability to be heart-centered. As a result, we are unable to manifest our true desires.

Any time you feel a contraction in your body or in your breathing, chances are you are moving into judgment. At that moment you can choose to stay in the ego's world of grief and trauma—or you can choose to connect with your own divinity, release your judgments, and begin to heal. When you do, you create a space for Grace to enter, and for your intentions to manifest.

- Remember that just as each of us is divine, each one of us also has the capacity for every human thought, feeling, and behavior. The most troubled individual you know has the capacity for deep love and compassion, and a desire for peace, love, and happiness. And you have within you the capacity to think, feel, and act in the most disturbing ways. Our world is a level playing field in which all of us share the same gifts and limitations—because within our human experience we are all connected to the Divine One Heart.

- When you feel a contraction in your body, take a few healing breaths and place your consciousness in your heart. Become aware of your feelings of judgment, and allow yourself the humor of being human. Remember that you are safe and loved. From this place it will become easier to drop your judgments.

## Forgiveness

Just as holding and releasing judgment is a function of the ego, forgiveness is a gift of the heart. Without it you can never truly be free of judgment. Forgiveness transforms the negativity of judgment so that it simply no longer exists.

Resistance to forgiveness holds our judgments in place and keeps us stuck in any number of ego defense patterns including victimhood, martyrdom, self-pity, shame, and domination. As with our judgments, when we resist forgiveness we choose grief and trauma over our ability to be divine co-creators of our intentions.

There is always a need for self-forgiveness. Without it we become our own abusers, continually berating, shaming, or otherwise putting ourselves in unhealthy situations. Any situation that triggers you to hold onto the illusion that you are separate from the Divine is an opportunity to choose to forgive yourself.

Without exception, realizing any intention requires some measure of forgiveness. Surprised? It's simple, really. If there was no need to forgive, the object of your intention would already be yours. When you forgive, you clear the lower frequencies that bind you to a person or situation in negativity, and generate a higher resonance that makes it possible for you to change and grow, and for your dream to become real.

Forgiveness also:

- expands your imagination beyond what you can know and expect,
- triggers compassion and transcendence,
- makes your choices more free and powerful,
- helps you to take responsibility for yourself,

- brings peace to your heart so you have the power to see how peace can unfold in our world.

If you still sense some resistance to forgiveness, these techniques may help:

- Ask yourself this question: What if everything you have ever done—no matter how illogical or extreme—was an effort to feel the connection, safety, and love we all long for? From this place can you be gentle enough with yourself to forgive yourself for the times you were not acting from your divinity? Are you willing to recognize your own divinity?

- Now consider someone else you need to forgive. What if everything he or she has ever done was also an effort to feel the connection, safety, and love we all long for? Can you see yourself in the person who has hurt you? Remember that you, too, are capable of every human thought, feeling, and behavior, just as he or she is. Even if you have never hurt another in the way you have been hurt, acknowledge that under certain threatening circumstances you might be capable of doing the same thing. Are you willing to see the divinity in the other person? Can you soften enough to allow yourself to forgive?

- Remember that forgiveness is the key to your freedom to heal and grow. Begin to see the situation you need to forgive as an opportunity for healing and growth, and allow your heart to find gratitude for that opportunity. As gratitude fills your heart allow love, joy, and wonder to arise.

- What do you want more than your grief and trauma? How firmly can you stand at the edge of your imagination and dream a new, more expansive dream for yourself? Can you allow forgiveness to help you realize that dream?

## Heart Resonance

Our judgments and resistance to forgiveness, and the ego stories that arise from them, separate us from our divinity and are too often the focus of our thoughts and energy. As a result we generate a lower vibrational frequency that interferes in a powerful way with our ability to receive. Your human gift of choice gives you the power to choose to lift out of your ego stories and release beliefs that do not support your healing.

When you are free of your stories and negative beliefs, you can begin to choose higher and higher states of resonance through gratitude, love, joy, and wonder. When you notice the things you have to be grateful for, the energy of love begins to fill your heart; joy inevitably follows, and then the wonder of discovering the many miracles and gifts that surround you flows easily.

Any time you find yourself caught in the negative energy of your ego stories, take a moment to focus on your heart, and turn your attention to the things you have to be grateful for. Notice how your heart expands as it fills with love, and celebrate the energy of joy and wonder that follows. If you find you are unable to feel joy in any given moment, try to at least find the wonder in knowing that your healing is already unfolding.

## Receiving and Harnessing Grace

When you connect to your own divinity through gratitude, love, joy, and wonder your heart vibrates at the highest resonance, and you become an attractor of Grace. It is yours to claim, receive, and embody any moment you choose to do so.

Sadly, many of us have been indoctrinated with the notion that it is better to give than to receive, or that we are unworthy of receiving gifts from other people or from the Divine. We may have experienced some kind of trauma around receiving that left us feeling deeply hurt, abandoned, or humiliated. Our experiences may even have led us to believe there's a price to pay when we receive good things from others; we assume that nothing is offered without strings attached. Often in the face of this kind of wounding we attempt to protect ourselves from pain by choosing not to receive at all.

The first step toward expanding your ability to receive is to notice that feelings of unworthiness are a form of judgment toward yourself. When you can make the choice to step out of that ego story and into your own divinity, you will be more open to receiving Grace and all the other gifts life has to offer.

It's also important to understand that receiving is the critical link in the infinite cycle of love and abundance. The truth is that without a receiver there is no true giving.

As you increase your capacity to receive you will discover that the line between giving and receiving begins to blur, until you come to know that there is no distinction in the unending circuit of giving and receiving—there is only the energy of love.

Developing your ability to choose your inner experience moment by moment is an essential part of receiving and harnessing Grace. Being fully present in the journey of being a spiritual adventurer means that you honor your choice to be in your heart in gratitude, love, joy, and wonder in as many moments as possible throughout the day. In these resonance states, receiving and harnessing Grace becomes more and more certain. The more you choose those higher states of resonance, the more you will be connected with the Divine One Heart and able to receive the miracles and gifts of connectedness, transcendence, and manifestation.

# Choose to Heal:
## Enhance the Power of
## The Grace Process

The TGP Formula is the foundation of your journey to heal with The Grace Process. What follows are strategies you can use to deepen your understanding of the formula, and help make your spiritual practice an integral part of your daily life.

### Place Your Consciousness in Your Heart

There are many beautiful writings about the importance of living from your heart. It's widely acknowledged that it's an essential component of healing and growth. Even the scientists agree (well, many of them do), as neurocardiologists have now demonstrated that our hearts have their own intelligence. I have found that whatever healing I need to do, if I consciously set my intention to be in my heart, it will do the rest.

But sometimes it's difficult to shift your energy from your brain and your ego to the softness of your heart. Whether you are engaged in everyday activities or working with your meditation practice, the following questions will help you identify where your energy lies.

- **Is my breathing contracted or expanded?** When you are breathing shallowly you are more likely to be triggered by your ego. When you are breathing deeply from your diaphragm it is easier to be in your heart.

- **Do I feel contracted or expanded in my body?** When you feel tension or contraction in your body, chances are you are in your ego. When you feel relaxed and expanded in your body, chances are you are in your heart.

- **Am I in judgment, or resisting forgiveness?** When you are judging or resisting forgiveness for yourself, another person, or the situation in which you find yourself, you are in survival mode and your ego is in charge.

- **Am I living in my ego stories?** If you find those stories replaying themselves endlessly in your mind, you're living in the world of your ego, not in your heart.

- **How easy is it for me to find gratitude, love, joy, and wonder in this moment?** The easier it is to experience these states of being and feeling, the more grounded you are in your heart. Practicing gratitude, love, joy, and wonder activates the highest resonance of your heart.

- **Am I experiencing heart stillness?** Try to find that quiet place inside, not only when you're meditating, but at any time throughout the day. If you're unable to find it no matter what is unfolding around you, your ego has taken over.

If you find it difficult to be in heart consciousness whenever you choose, whether you are performing a task or interacting with another person, take the time to be fully present in gratitude, love, joy, and wonder for your circumstances or for the person in front of you. Your experience of heart consciousness will be accelerated. In your meditation practice, calling up those emotions is like a conduit for attaining heart consciousness more quickly. From this place it is much easier to become quiet, to drop into the silence, and to listen to the wisdom of your heart.

## Look for Miracles and Gifts throughout Your Day

Every day, bring your intentions for healing into your awareness and ask the Divine One Heart to enchant you with miracles and gifts throughout your day. When you see them arise, you will know for sure that you are supported in manifesting what you desire. Remember, though, that you are the co-creator of everything you experience. It follows that you are also the co-creator of miracles and gifts. The Divine One Heart is eager to match your highest resonance. Your job is to choose to:

- keep your consciousness in your heart;

- experience the divinity in every person, situation, and circumstance you encounter;

- embrace *everything* you experience as a miracle or gift supporting you in the knowing that you are seen, heard, and connected with the Divine One Heart.

What do I mean by "miracles and gifts"? They're the unexpected moments of beauty that you take time to notice, or the surprise happy endings when you thought you were headed for trouble. A gift can be as simple as a puppy bringing you a ball to throw, reminding you to take a break from your computer; a miracle can be the love, joy, and wonder you feel when you remember to be grateful when your favorite song comes on the radio while you're stuck in a traffic jam. Miracles and gifts also come in the form of what may at first appear to be adversity. When we look deeply, beyond our ego stories, we can choose to see our greatest challenges as our greatest opportunities.

Here are few examples of the miracles and gifts I recently received in a single day. I started the day feeling the pleasure of taking time to stretch, breathe, and connect with my divinity before I got out of bed in the morning. I entered the bathroom, chose an angel card from the shelf, and laughed out loud at how appropriate its message was. Seeing the toothpaste tube almost empty, I praised the toothpaste fairies for helping me squeeze out just enough to brush my teeth. As I waited in a long line when I was rushed for time, I took the time to really see the divinity in the people around me, and was surprised by a sweet exchange with another shopper—and then found that I had all the time I needed to get where I was going. Feeling a bit stuck in my writing, I looked outside my window to find a mother seagull teaching her offspring to fly; when I allowed myself to notice the wonder of the scene, I was inspired to continue my writing. In the midst of an ongoing state of emergency due to raging fires overtaking my community, I was able to remain calm and centered, grieve for the devastation, hold compassion for the victims, and be in wonder about the opportunities for healing that might unfold for each of us and our city.

As you honor the miracles and gifts that emerge all around you, you'll find that your resonance remains steady and your sense of connectedness, well-being, and Grace will flow.

## Remember that *Everything* You Experience Is an Opportunity to Heal

When you find yourself facing a challenge, and notice you're feeling angry or sad or frustrated by it, bring your attention back to your heart and know that everything that happens to you, without exception, is an opportunity for you to heal. It may appear that your circumstances are proof that your intention for healing is not, will not, and can never be manifest. But that simply is not the case.

Remember the research on the holographic field? Your intention and what you desire is reflected everywhere in the universe. Through your work with your intentions you know that your healing is already unfolding—what you desire already exists. And so, those challenges you face are simply the Divine One Heart showing you where you need to heal an old pattern or an old way of being in the world. It's up to you to look at everything you experience as an opportunity to release those old patterns, those old ego stories, and move instead into heart resonance.

Albert Einstein, a mystic, genius and scientist, said, "There are only two ways to look at your life. One is as if nothing is a miracle. The other is as if everything is a miracle."

His friend, Nobel laureate Rabindranath Tagore, offered this teaching on faith:

A spiritual master in India wanted to build a temple and made plans to do so even though the master had no funds for the project. One of his anxious students pleaded, "Oh Master, but where will the money come from?"

The master replied, "From wherever it is now, of course!"

When you question whether what you are experiencing is serving your healing, consider this: What if the Divine One Heart has heard your request, and is offering something that looks like an enticement into an old suffer-and-struggle pattern as a way of asking you, *Are you really, really sure you want to change this pattern in your life? Because if you are, here's an opportunity right now to embrace your intention, drop your resistance, and receive a new way of being, healing, and growing.*

## Find Humor and Cosmic Winks in Your Day

Humor is an elegant tool for transcending your ego and shifting your resonance to gratitude, love, joy, and wonder. When a challenge arises, the sooner you can find the humor in it—no matter how ironic the situation might be—the sooner you'll be able to release the ego story you've attached to it. When you move through your day with the light energy of humor, your intentions will manifest more easily—and you'll be more prepared to recognize them when they show up.

Here's what I do when I find myself believing that things are not going the way they should. First, I bless myself in gratitude that I am aware I'm caught in an ego story, and that I've managed to bring my attention back to the present moment. Then I bless my ego in gratitude for giving me a red flag that I might be resisting my healing. Most of the time I can find humor in the irony of how uniquely and exceedingly clever my ego is in distracting me.

For example, sometimes I hear that ego voice in my head saying, "Hey, I already healed that issue in my life. This must be the other person's fault, not mine!"

That's when I have to laugh and realize that what's showing up in my reality is a cosmic wink from the Divine One Heart saying, "Your intention has been heard, but you still have more to learn. Here's an opportunity to get your attention and speed you on your journey."

That's right. If it's showing up in my reality it's another opportunity for me to learn more forgiveness and deeper states of GLJW on my healing journey—and an opportunity to have a good chuckle along the way.

## Love Yourself with Boundaries

The formula for harnessing Grace requires that you love yourself with boundaries. It's essential that you make a commitment to take care of yourself by putting your own healthy emotional, physical, and spiritual needs first. That includes setting personal boundaries. However, many of us are still strongly programmed by culture, religion, and codependency that love requires self-sacrifice, putting others' needs before our own.

Setting boundaries comes from honoring the gift of your emotions. When you accept your emotions with an open heart, and avoid clouding them with judgment, they provide a wealth of signals that will help you take care of yourself. Loving feelings let you know that all is well and that you are taking care of yourself in the moment. Angry feelings tell you that either you, another person, or a situation may not be meeting your needs for respect, self-determination, or reciprocation of your love. Fearful feelings warn you that you may need to protect yourself in some way. Sad feelings are a signal that the form of something you valued has been lost to you in some way. On a deeper level, every emotion is a form of either love or fear. Love is a sign you are living in your heart. Fear, in the absence of true danger, lets you know you are living in your ego.

Whatever your emotions are signaling to you, when you feel them arise it is important to use your breath to help you stay grounded in your body and remain in heart consciousness. From that place you can use the wealth of information available in those emotions to make healthy choices about the boundaries you need to create to love yourself well.

Asserting your boundaries is a great manifestation tool for co-creation. It clears away negative attachments and circumstances that interfere with calling in what you desire for yourself. Boundaries are your vibrational language for saying, *I am taking responsibility for myself. I am supporting my needs and desires. I matter, and what I desire matters.*

## Stay on the Path Toward Receiving Grace

Much of the energy of the ego is devoted to maintaining the status quo. It seeks to maintain control over your life, keep you from living in heart consciousness, and block you from receiving the function of your desires. Judgment and resistance to forgiveness are powerful tools the ego engages in to accomplish those goals. And they're very effective—*if* you allow them to distract you from your path toward healing.

Choose instead to remain focused on the healing you desire. Each time you find yourself feeling unworthy, unlovable, better than, less than, entitled, depressed, anxious, or any other sign that the ego is invoking the illusion of separateness, choose instead to bring your attention to your heart, and call upon feelings of gratitude, love, joy, and wonder.

It's important not to demonize or separate yourself from your ego, but simply to be aware of its distractions so you can easily shift into your heart when you feel judgment and resistance to forgiveness arise. If you do, you will remain open to the energy of Grace.

# The Grace Process
## Meditation Practices

The Grace Process Meditation Practices are tools for healing the wound of separation, activating heart consciousness, strengthening your ability to receive healing, and harnessing the experience of Grace. You can work with the companion CD for this book, *The Grace Process: Meditations, Volume I*, available on our website or through most major retail outlets, or with other CDs available on our website at www.TheGraceProcess.com. You can also incorporate TGP into your own meditation practice.

The companion CD offers two meditations. The first, "Opening Your Heart to Receiving," is a ten-minute practice you can use to center yourself in your heart throughout the day. "Receiving Heart Wisdom" is a twenty-minute meditation you can use to move more deeply into the process of releasing judgments, opening to forgiveness and receiving the healing you desire for yourself and our world.

More than 2,500 studies have proven the many benefits of meditating. Whether you use the companion CD or incorporate TGP into your regular meditation practice, here are some of the benefits you will experience:

- You will feel the safety, peace, and wisdom that flow from exploring heart stillness.

- You'll tune your body to the highest resonance for harnessing Grace.

- You will allow your heart to be the engine of your experience.

- You will remember that you are connected to the Divine and that you have all the resources you need to support your healing.

- You'll receive healing insights and energy shifts that let you know you are already manifesting your intention.

## The Grace Trinity

A hallmark of the Grace Process Meditation Practices is the Grace Trinity. With this practice you invoke a pyramid of resonance created by your Soul, Spirit, and Higher Self, and you expand your experience of connectedness with your divinity. You can choose to work with this trinity of energy whether you are using the companion CD or doing your own meditation practice. You can also use it when you first wake up in the morning, just before you go to sleep, or whenever you choose to take a quiet moment in the middle of your day.

Here's how:

1. Focus on expanding your breathing.
2. Place your consciousness in your heart in whatever way feels right to you. Your heart will know what to do.
3. Bring your intention for healing into your awareness.
4. Bring in the energy of your Soul, and sense its presence to your left. For the purposes of this work, your Soul represents your sacred feminine energy. Your Soul is that quiet part of you that remembers the lessons you came here to learn and the reason for the journey of this lifetime. Your Soul is that part of you that knows how to receive.
5. Bring in the energy of your Spirit, and sense its presence to your right. Your Spirit is a reflection of your sacred masculine energy. Your Spirit is that part of you that inspires you and wills you to action from love, not fear.
6. Remember that when Soul and Spirit are in balance it is easier to integrate to your Higher Self.
7. Bring in the energy of your Higher Self, and sense it's presence just above you. Your Higher Self is that part of you that is directly connected to the Divine. Your Higher Self wants you to have the most elegant journey possible.
8. Step into the resonance of the Trinity. Remember that you are not alone, that through these sacred aspects of

yourself you are connected to the Divine One Heart, and that you have all the resources you need for your healing journey.

**Meditative Practice:
Relationship with Grace
Trinity**

Higher Self

Self

Soul                    Spirit

## Infuse Your Grace Trinity with Heart Resonance (GLJW).

Your ability to harness the experience of Grace is co-created and strengthened when you ground the being and feeling states of gratitude, love, joy, and wonder into your body and into your meditations. When you take time to feel into what you have to be grateful for, feelings of love arise quite easily. When you combine states of gratitude and love, they naturally give rise to states of joy and wonder.

9.  While sitting within the resonance of the Grace Trinity, take a moment to think about all you have to be grateful for, and who and what you love in your life.

10. Notice how that gratitude and love expands, and what joy and wonder may unfold. If you're unable to touch into joy, remember at least that everything you experience is serving your healing.

11. Touch into the wonder of how your healing is already unfolding.

12. Now, take some time to listen to the wisdom of your heart and receive an experience of Grace in the form of a word, a phrase, an image, a deep sense of knowing, a body sensation, or any other form you become aware of.

## Your Own Meditation Practice

Here are a few guidelines for working with TGP in your regular meditation time:

1.  **Center and prepare yourself for meditation.** Begin with healing breath work, that is, slow diaphragmatic breathing. (A "Healing Breath Work" meditation is available on a companion CD for *The Stress Management Handbook: Strategies for Health and Inner Peace* available at www.TheGraceProcess.com.)

2.  **Place your consciousness in your heart.** Since the heart has its own intelligence, simply focus your awareness in your heart, and know that your heart knows what to do. If you're experiencing any tension or contraction in your body, your awareness is probably in your brain. You'll know your consciousness is in your heart when you feel relaxed and expanded in your body. Just relax and allow your heart to do the work.

3.  **Bring your intention for healing into your awareness.**

4.  **Work with your Grace Trinity.** With your consciousness in your heart and your intention for healing in your awareness, invoke your Grace Trinity by bringing in the energies of your Soul, Spirit, and Higher Self. Step into the resonance of these sacred aspects of yourself, and touch into the energies of gratitude, love, joy, and wonder.

5.  **Listen to the wisdom of your heart.** When you feel ready, allow yourself to drop into heart stillness and listen to the wisdom of your heart for insights related to the healing you are seeking. You will know that your insights are coming from your heart when you feel expanded and relaxed in your body.

6.  **Allow Grace to unfold.**

7. **Imagine your healing unfolding.** See yourself moving through your days with the healing you seek.

8. **Imagine healing unfolding in the world.** Remembering that whatever you choose to heal in yourself sets up a resonance for that healing to occur in the world, imagine a world full of people who have experienced the healing you seek.

# Your Daily TGP Plan

O ne of the reasons The Grace Process is such a powerful healing practice is that it is designed to become part of your life, to infuse your entire day with your highest heart resonance and the energy of Grace.

Here are some steps you can take to incorporate your TGP spiritual practice into your everyday living:

- **Schedule an hourly heart/breath check-in.** Practice centering yourself in your heart with a few healing breaths for just one or two minutes every hour until you find yourself in your heart naturally and often. You will notice a greater sense of healthy control, focus, and peace as well as the ability to choose your next healthy action. These check-ins allow you to become aware of whether you've been in your heart or your ego. Once aware, you can take a moment in time to choose to shift your consciousness to your heart, to focus on gratitude, love, joy, and wonder, or to simply look for the evidence in your day that your Higher Self is enchanting you with support. You can also take this time to remember your intention for healing, and to keep it in your awareness.

- **Attune yourself to your breathing and to your heart.** In addition to your hourly check-in, choose to practice healing breath work and to place your consciousness in your heart in as many moments as possible throughout the day. Developing a practice of remembering to choose heart consciousness again and again is the first step on your path to peace, freedom, and enlightenment.

- **Look for the miracles and gifts.** This might be the most powerful resonance shifter you will ever know. Ask your Higher Self to enchant you with miracles and gifts, and with every breath and heartbeat practice gratitude, love, joy, and wonder for all that shows up as you go through your day. Take time to reflect on how those miracles and gifts are assisting you in manifesting your intentions.

- **Find humor—and let your laughter loose.** There is humor everywhere, in yourself, others, nature and the Divine One Heart. If you hear yourself saying any version of "You've got to be sh!#%ting me...!!" about anything at all, I'm here to tell you, *yeup*, it's your ego talking. Your ego may be very clever in the resistance department, but your Higher Self is more clever in presenting you with situations that *really* get your attention—especially when you get really close to choosing your healing over your grief and trauma. I promise you, when times appear to get tough...those are the times when you've just gotta laugh!

- **Meditate.** Develop a regular practice based on TGP principles, or incorporate TGP into your existing practice. The companion CD, *The Grace Process: Meditations, Volume I* (available on our website or through retailers), offers you two guided meditation opportunities. One is just ten minutes long, the other is twenty minutes long. I suggest two ten-minute meditations each day or one longer one of twenty minutes. Whether in meditation or not, taking time to focus on your Grace Trinity from time to time throughout the day is a strong reminder that you are not alone, that you are connected to these divine aspects of yourself, and that you have all the resources you need for your healing journey.

- **Commit to keeping a Grace Experience Journal.** Yes, you've heard this advice before. But now try it with this twist. Every morning write down your reflections about the miracles and gifts you co-created and experienced the day before—no matter how big or small—then set your intentions for the current day. Start with a radiance of gratitude for all that unfolded the previous day. Notice how that gives rise to feelings of love, which give rise to feelings of joy, and then wonder. These states are always available to you when you find miracles and gifts in the seemingly smallest of insights and happenings. The next morning write down your reflections again. Soon you will be observing and experiencing the world all day, every day through the highest resonance of your heart.

- **Know that you are already healing.** You can be certain that from the moment you begin working with TGP you are creating a resonance for personal and global transformation. Remember that whatever you choose to heal in yourself sets up a resonance for that healing to occur in the world; when you are serving yourself, you are in service to the world as well. As you heal and grow it becomes easier for others to step into the river of healing and growth.

## The Ebbs and Flows of Receiving

Sometimes you will experience self-doubt, or a dip in your ability to hold gratitude, love, joy, and wonder in your heart. There are times when you will experience relative quiet, or seemingly slow times when it seems like your intentions are not manifesting and your healing is not unfolding in the way you expect it to, or in the timeframe you hoped for. Sometimes it even feels like the circumstance you are trying to heal is getting worse, or has been compounded by other complicating factors. Perhaps you're trying to heal some financial issues, and your car breaks down causing you another unexpected bill. Or maybe you're trying to love yourself with boundaries, but family members and clients are in crisis and wanting more and more of your help. These times are what I call "being in the ebb," like when an ocean wave recedes.

And then there are those times we all crave, when miracles and gifts in support of our healing unfold easily and elegantly. These times are what I call "being in the flow," like when an ocean wave is rushing to the shore with great energy and aliveness.

Because we tend to enjoy being in the flow so much, we have a tendency to judge the ebb times as negative experiences. We may end up activating our ego with judgment and negative self-talk. "I must be doing something wrong." "I'm not really being supported by the Divine." "I'm not good enough." And on it goes.

When this happens, be careful not to retreat into the distractions of the ego. Remember, a wave recedes so it can become part of the greater whole and move forward again.

Those times when you are in the ebb are when you need TGP practices the most. You can move through the experience without becoming contracted and retreating into your ego if you continue to commit to the following:

1. Recommit to your daily TGP practice for expanding your heart resonance.
2. Know that your healing began to unfold the moment you set your intention, and it will continue to unfold as long as you stay out of the melodrama of your stories.
3. Become aware of signs that you are attached to your ego stories and choose to lift out of them.
4. Give up your attachment to the form of your healing.
5. Give up your attachment to the timing of your healing.

6. Open to releasing deeper levels of judgment and embracing deeper levels of forgiveness.
7. Look for cosmic winks from the Divine One Heart and find the humor in remembering that *everything* you experience is in service to your healing.

# Part III

# Deepening Your Study and Practice

*The very purpose of our life is to seek happiness.... The very motion of our life is towards happiness. We can never obtain peace in the outer world until we make peace with ourselves.*

—His Holiness the Dalai Lama

# The Grace Process
## Services and Offerings

Lori Leyden, Ph.D., M.B.A., has pioneered The Grace Process (TGP), a healing method based on the power of heart resonance. Her approach is grounded in energy psychology, neurocardiology, and quantum physics, as well as the great wisdom traditions.

Dr. Leyden offers services for individuals and groups seeking to deepen and expand their spiritual journeys. Her clients include new and long-time seekers, healing arts professionals, business and community leaders, humanitarians, and philanthropists. TGP has been used by many to overcome emotional, physical, and spiritual traumas as well as family, relationship, self-esteem, work, and health issues.

Using TGP practices enables you to be in service to your own healing and healing for the world at the same time. This approach is for you if you choose to commit to:

- Creating healing for yourself and our world.
- Transcending your ego and lifting out of the melodrama of your stories.
- Engaging in radical practices for releasing judgments, embracing forgiveness, and exploring the power of gratitude, love, joy, and wonder.
- Connecting more deeply with the wisdom of your heart.
- Honoring your humanness and your divinity with fun and humor.

Dr. Leyden offers a variety of opportunities to support and deepen your personal TGP practice.

- **Individual Coaching Sessions:** (Available by phone or in person.)
- **Train the Trainer Sessions:** (Available by phone or in person.) This work is specifically for healing arts practitioners, coaches, workshop leaders, and other spiritual growth professionals who want to experience TGP and learn how they can incorporate TGP into their work with clients.

- **Grace Process Study Groups:** (Available as a teleconference or in person.) Study groups generally meet once a week for six weeks. We create a space that is sacredly playful yet profound, one that honors both the individual and the power of the group in their ability to co-create the healing we all seek. You'll come to the first meeting with an intention of what you would like to heal or achieve. Each week you'll learn more about how to apply TGP practices, and throughout the week you'll look for the evidence—sometimes small miracles and gifts, sometimes large ones—that support you in your healing. You'll learn how to lift out of your "story" and heal any limiting patterns or beliefs that are nagging you or holding you back from living your best life. You'll experience more of your intuition and a deeper knowing that you are not alone, as your spirituality comes alive in everyday living.

- **Spa for the Soul Immersion Experience:** This work is uniquely designed for individuals or small groups (four people or less), and takes place over a two- to five-day period. Participants learn TGP practices, immerse themselves in an environment in which they can "live" the work, and co-create transformational experiences to accelerate growth and healing.

- **Heart–Centered Business Consulting:** TGP practices have proven effective in a variety of forms in the workplace. Whether through individual mentoring or group work, TGP allows business owners, executives, and staff to meet challenges in the workplace with peace of mind, an open heart, and increased focus, effectiveness, and creativity.

- **Retreats and Workshops**: Lori is available to bring TGP to you if you would like to sponsor a retreat or workshop in your area.

- **Conferences**: Invite Dr. Leyden to bring TGP to your conference as a speaker or to facilitate a seminar. Her insights are welcomed by healing practitioners and entrepreneurs as well as spiritual and community leaders.

- **Keynote Speaker**: An inspirational speaker, Dr. Leyden has addressed more than two hundred professional and general audiences in major cities in the United States.

Lori welcomes your input, inquiries and feedback about your experiences with The Grace Process.

## Contact Information:

www.TheGraceProcess.com
Lori@TheGraceProcess.com

*"I experienced Lori Leyden's "Magic" on the last day of the ACEP conference in New Mexico last May. Her seminar called "The Transforming Power of Grace" was without question transforming.*

*"Saturated, after four days of information and training, I did not anticipate being impressed, let alone profoundly moved as I walked into Lori's seminar. What I experienced in those two hours has continued to feed me energetically for the past eight months. Lori's 'The Grace Process' is a*

*spiritual practice that has assisted me in blending my psychotherapy practice much more effectively with the concepts of energy psychology. But it was the experiential aspect of her seminar that has stayed with me so strongly. In her seminar group practices, Lori merges a room full of strangers together into a 'Oneness' that is so precious it is life changing. This happening is beyond word description, one literally must experience it. The addition of this incredible woman should be a standard of any Energy Psychology Conference."*

–Liza Bell, L.C.S.W.

# The Grace Process™
## Flower and Gem Essence

The Grace Process™ (TGP) Flower and Gem Essence is a unique, vibrationally infused combination of nine powerful essences including Andean orchids from Machu Picchu, pink lotus and other flowers from Santa Barbara, and citrine and azurite-malachite gemstones. Each bottle has been individually created using a base of activated healing waters gathered from sacred sites around the world.

### Divine Alchemy

Flower and gem essences have been used throughout time by indigenous cultures. Described as "tinctures of liquid consciousness," vibrational essences carry high harmonic frequencies that work according to the principles of resonance. They increase and accelerate your ability to receive the healing you seek, and are compatible with any other healing modalities you wish to use. The Grace Process™ Flower and Gem Essence will strengthen your TGP practice and raise your resonance for opening and expanding your heart to experience Grace.

## Benefits

Our essence formula is made from a selection of impeccable, therapeutic quality Star Essences (www.StarFlowerEssences.com) that support TGP practices by:

- transmuting and transforming judgments and negativity;
- healing and grounding your energy field for optimal mental, physical, emotional, and spiritual health;
- attaining new levels of connectedness with yourself, others, nature, and the Divine—the energy for peace in our world;
- amplifying higher resonance energies of gratitude, love, joy, and wonder;
- magnifying your heart energy for dreaming and co-creation;
- balancing your divine feminine and masculine energies so you can more easily integrate to your divine self.

## Dosage & Usage

- With conscious intention, take 4 drops or one spray at a time.

- Using the essence regularly and consistently harmonizes you to its resonance.

- Use upon rising and retiring, during meditation, and throughout the day as you are inspired to.

- Drops may be taken orally, placed in drinking or bath water, or on the skin.

- Spray may be used on the skin or acupressure points, and for space clearing, altar activation, feng shui, or in ceremonies and rituals.

- Spray lightly on face for rejuvenation and as a makeup refresher.

- Animals enjoy a gentle spray or a few drops in their drinking water.

- Plants and flowers are healthier and last longer with drops or spray.

100% safe and natural for everyone including
children, animals, and plants.
Preserved with alcohol.
Spray contains essential oils.

### Order TGP Flower and Gem Essences at:
www.TheGraceProcess.com
Lori@TheGraceProcess.com

# Create Global Healing

*Opening hearts, healing our children, healing our world*

*"Our desire is to make a significant contribution to bringing about a collective "heart" shift that results in global peace and healing. Our vision is for adults and children worldwide to connect with each other in a spirit of 'oneness,' and an unbroken circuit of giving and receiving so that we can all participate in co-creating a better future for ourselves and our world."*

–Lori Leyden, Founder, Create Global Healing.

Dr. Lori Leyden was inspired to establish Create Global Healing, a 501(c)3 nonprofit corporation, after her life-changing experience working with widow and orphan genocide survivors in Rwanda, where she leads trauma healing and reconciliation programs for high school orphans and orphan heads of households (children raising other children). Here in the United States she conducts and supports heart-centered leadership development programs for middle-school students and humanitarians.

## Our focus:

- working with traumatized orphan genocide survivors;
- creating inspirational healing and heart-opening experiences that connect orphans around the world, students in the United States, and humanitarians;
- creating alliances with other organizations that share our visions and values.

## Our mission:

We believe that everyone is entitled to live with dignity, peace, and hope, and that the promise for peace in our world lies in nurturing our children to become global citizens and compassionate leaders. By focusing on trauma healing for orphans and by developing opportunities for United States students and humanitarians to connect with orphans around the world, Create Global Healing seeks to shine a beacon of light on one of the greatest human gifts that can unite us all—the power and resilience of the human heart. We believe that global healing will take place through compassionate, heart-centered experiences that foster the understanding that we are all connected.

For more information about Create Global Healing programs and opportunities to partner with us, please visit our website at:

www.CreateGlobalHealing.org.

A portion of the proceeds from this book will be donated to Create Global Healing.

# Expressions of Gratitude for
# The Grace Process

*There is no path to happiness. Happiness is the Path.*
–Lao-Tse

*"Lori is a great gift to the field of Energy Psychology. Her work truly transforms the people who come to her. She is a talented counselor, teacher and innovator. Her workshop provided a transcendental experience for all who attended. One of the amazing qualities about Lori is that she truly walks her talk. She radiates love and acceptance. She shares her knowledge and talent in the US as well as in Africa where her work has made a difference in so many lives."*

–Gloria Arenson, M.S., M.F.T., D.C.E.P., past president,
Association for Comprehensive Energy Psychology

*"I experienced Lori Leyden's "Magic" on the last day of the ACEP conference in New Mexico last May. Her seminar called "The Transforming Power of Grace" was without question transforming.*

*"Saturated, after four days of information and training, I did not anticipate being impressed, let alone profoundly moved as I walked into Lori's seminar. What I experienced in those two hours has continued to feed me energetically for the past eight months. Lori's 'The Grace Process' is a spiritual practice that has assisted me in blending my psychotherapy practice much more effectively with the concepts of energy psychology. But it was the experiential aspect of her seminar that has stayed with me so strongly. In her seminar group practices, Lori merges a room full of strangers together into a 'Oneness' that is so precious it is life changing. This happening is beyond word description, one literally must experience it. The addition of this incredible woman should be a standard of any Energy Psychology Conference."*

–Liza Bell, L.C.S.W.

*"For years after my trauma, I didn't believe that I would ever get back to a place of calm within myself, or that I could ever feel happy and healthy again. I was stuck. My depression, anxiety, negative self-talk, and addictions had frozen my life and my career. But Lori and The Grace Process provided the nurturing I needed to forgive myself and to forgive others. Releasing myself from so much shame and humiliation has opened up my heart.*

*"Through the process we laughed and we cried, but even in the difficult moments, the excitement that was building inside of me helped me move through it and catapulted me forward in my healing. I feel safe inside myself now and I believe in myself again! I am not perfect, and sometimes I waiver, but I've been given this beautiful new beginning and so many personal and*

*professional opportunities are coming into my life! I know that this has happened because of the incredible journey that Lori guided me through. I have grabbed the reins and am living life again."*

–S. J., Actor, Playwright

*"Lori's work is not only insightful but gracefully transformational. Previous therapy had only scratched the surface of the inner struggle on the lessons that I need to learn in this lifetime. Truly compassionate and connected, working with Lori in The Grace Process has allowed me to connect with my truer self."*

–Nicole Olsen, Doctor of Chiropractic

*"Lori is a highly intuitive facilitator whose work is profound and transformative. She practices what she preaches, and as a result she has faced some of life's most difficult challenges with dignity, grace, humor, and integrity."*

–S. E. Fox, transformational educator and author of
*Visual Journaling*

*"Lori is the real deal—and I've done it all. She's a fabulous spiritual life coach connecting you to your own inner healer."*

–Mimi Donaldson, speaker, consultant, author of
*Bless Your Stress: It Means You're Still Alive* and *Negotiating for Dummies*

"*The Grace Process is extremely powerful and puts you in contact with the many resources we all have within to heal ourselves and our lives. Lori is an incredible guide helping to clear away the old outmoded programming, leaving you feeling deeply connected with yourself. In one session I was able to change my life completely.*"

—A.B., holistic healer

"*The Grace process is very real and goes very deep. Lori is an amazing facilitator. The Grace Process showed me a very clear vision of my future that I carry with me. I can see old ways of being and patterns virtually falling away. I now have an effortless roadmap in a very clear vision to what was once just an ideal future.*"

—Deborah Stuart, president, Oxygen Research Institute

"*The Grace Process draws on the energy of ancient ritual, connecting people back to their spiritual heritage - giving them a greater sense of unity and oneness. ...The Grace Process sets up a very high level, heart chakra breakthrough process where people can really own their own divinity.*

—Galexis, channeled spirit guide

"*Lori entices us to examine our perceptions of reality with humor and compassion. She reflects our divinity back to us, elegantly meets us where we are, and lovingly inspires us to vision and carry out our dreams for ourselves, our loved ones, our work, and our world.*"

—Carol Long, artist

*"I have the courage to live again. "*

—J. K., two-time cancer survivor.


*"The thing I found most healing about working with Lori was her calming, loving presence and unconditional acceptance."*

—Dean McCormick, Lawyer


*"Dr. Leyden is a uniquely experienced, authentically gifted spiritual teacher for those sincerely searching for core level transformation."*

—Warren Benning, M.Div., minister

# About Lori Leyden, Ph.D., M.B.A.

In 2003 Lori Leyden was reflecting on the next step on her soul path. Within the space of eight weeks she left her home, marriage, and business of fourteen years, endured two emergency surgeries, and had a near death experience that ultimately prompted her to ask for divine guidance. She followed that guidance from one coast to the other to find her new home and her new work—The Grace Process, a spiritual practice for heart-centered living.

Lori holds a doctorate in Health and Human Services with a concentration in psychoneuroimmunology, and a masters degree in Business Administration with a concentration in management. With more than thirty years experience in the fields of psychotherapy, business, and spiritual growth, Dr. Leyden is a uniquely qualified author, workshop leader, business consultant, and humanitarian. After working with widow and orphan genocide survivors in Rwanda, she developed Create Global Healing, a nonprofit organization committed to developing heart-centered leadership programs for orphans in war torn countries, and for students, humanitarians, and philanthropists in the United States.

Dr. Leyden has been featured in PBS's *Healthy Living* series and on more than one hundred radio and television shows, and in numerous magazines and newspapers including *Natural Health, New Woman, The Daily Word, Travel Life*, and *Celebrity Bulletin*. As a diplomate of the American Psychotherapy Association she was the first spirituality columnist for the association's professional journal, *Annals*.

She is the author of *The Grace Process Guidebook: Receiving the Healing You Yearn For* and *The Stress Management Handbook: Strategies for Health and Inner Peace*, available in English, Spanish, Arabic, and Korean.

Lori currently facilitates healing work with The Grace Process, sharing the heart of what she's learned using humor, life stories, and interactive exercises. She radiates the joy and inner peace she has found for herself, and sparks our imagination for the possibilities of achieving world peace through inner peace and outer good works. She resides in Santa Barbara, California.